THE

SEER

McDougal & Associates
Servants of Christ and Stewards of the
Mysteries of God

THE

SEER

BY

APOSTLE ROBERT DELGADO

Published by:

McDougal & Associates
18896 Greenwell Springs Road
Greenwell Springs, LA 70739
www.ThePublishedWord.com

McDougal & Associates is dedicated to spreading the Gospel of the Lord Jesus Christ to as many people as possible in the shortest time possible.

ISBN: 978-1-950398-80-5

Printed on demand in the U.S., the U.K., Australia, and the UAE
For Worldwide Distribution

DEDICATION

I dedicate this book to the Person who has been with me since the foundations of the world. He was with me through my turbulent growing-up years, especially when He told me, "When you needed a father, I was there. When you needed a mother, I was there. When you needed a brother or sister, I was there." He was there all the time. He has been with me through my pastorship (pastoring the same church for thirty-nine years—All Nations Church in Rosenberg, Texas) and my calling to my apostleship to the nations, all by the will of the Father and not the will of man. That special Person is none other than the precious and mighty Holy Spirit of God!

Acknowledgments

First, I want to thank my dear friends—Dr. Thomas Elias and his precious wife, Dr. Gracie—for their encouragement for the publishing of this book. May God richly bless them and prosper them.

Second, I want to thank my dear wife, Prophetess Linda Delgado, for being an eyewitness of the prophetic words and revelations God has given me.

CONTENTS

FOREWORD BY THOMAS ELIAS

I am delighted to write about *THE SEER*, the short book written by Pastor Robert Delgado, my dear friend and servant of God. I have known Robert since 2015 when I was a chaplain at the Houston Methodist Sugar Land Hospital, where he was a patient. I have had the opportunity to minister in his church—All Nations Worship Center, Richmond, Texas. My wife and I traveled with Robert and his wife, Linda, twice to minister to the people in the southern states of Tabasco, Campeche, Yucatan, and Quintana Roo of the great country of Mexico.

THE SEER is a compilation of the author's experiences during the many years of his pastoral and prophetic ministries. It talks about his dreams and visions and how they came to pass—sometimes after he had waited patiently for many years. His sixteen years (1995-2011) of ministry as the Coordinator for Spanish Christian Programming for Latin America through Trinity Broadcasting Network (TBN) at Channel 14 in Houston, Texas was a fulfillment of a dream God gave him in 1984.

THE SEER talks about spiritual, physical, and social healing in the Latin American countries and the United States. Through all this, Robert was in the midst of spiritual warfare, keenly aware that *"our struggle is not against flesh and blood, but against the rulers, against the authorities, against the powers of this dark world and against the spiritual forces of evil in the heavenly realms"* (Ephesians 6:12).

When you read through these pages, I urge you to experience the God who fulfills His redemptive and healing work among the people of this world. He uses faithful people like Robert Delgado, who are willing to be submissive to His will and His plan. I encourage you to read this book and understand God's move to fulfill His sovereign purposes through the ages—past, present, and future. To God be the glory!

Thomas Elias, Ph.D.

Pastor and author

(Retired engineer and university professor)

THUS SPEAKS THE LORD GOD OF
ISRAEL, SAYING: "WRITE IN A BOOK
FOR YOURSELF ALL THE WORDS THAT
I HAVE SPOKEN TO YOU."

— Jeremiah 30:2

INTRODUCTION

(Formerly in Israel, when a man went to inquire of God, he spoke thus: "Come, let us go to the seer"; for he who is now called a prophet was formerly called a seer.) 1 Samuel 9:9

The Bible speaks of a prophet as a seer. Prophets were called seers before they were called prophets. What is a seer? It is a person chosen by God to reveal things that He is doing in the present or is going to do in the future. Prophets see things before others see them. Prophets, or seers, played a prominent role in Jewish life. They were the conduits between God and man:

> *Surely the LORD God does nothing,*
> *Unless He reveals His secret to His*
> *servants the prophets.* Amos 3:7

I strongly believe that God does not want His people, be it Israel or the Church of Jesus Christ, to be in the dark about things that are happening or that are going to happen in the future. Consider these passages: :

> *And the LORD said, "Shall I hide from*
> *Abraham what I am doing?"*
> Genesis 18:17

> *But you, brethren, are not in darkness,*
> *so that this Day [the Rapture] should*
> *overtake you as a thief. You are all sons*
> *of light and sons [children] of the day.*
> *We are not of the night nor of darkness.*
> 1 Thessalonians 5:4-5

The Church will surely be warned of the return of our Lord Jesus Christ for His people. God knows the future. He knows the end from the beginning, and throughout

Bible history, He has revealed His plans and purposes through His seers. These were people like Abraham, Joseph, Moses, Samuel, the major and minor prophets, the Apostle John, and Jesus Himself. They were all used to reveal what God was doing in the Earth and what He was going to do in the future in the affairs of men, His people (Israel), and the Church, to bring about His plans and purposes.

Do we have seers today? Yes, we do! I know firsthand. On the last Saturday of April of 1996, I was asking Jesus why I had never had a revelation of Him, even though I had believed in Him without seeing Him. Then, on the first Saturday of May, I had a dream. Before I saw anything, I heard a rushing mighty wind and a roar of mighty waters (like Niagara Falls).

After that, I saw a very bright light engulfing me. I looked up and saw Jesus in the clouds. He looked just like we imagine Him. He was wearing a bright white robe with a light blue sash across His chest. His hair was long and brown. His face was a bright light, and His arms were outstretched.

Immediately, I lifted my arms to fly to Him, but He said, "Not yet." I didn't feel bad because He said that.

Then, everything darkened and once again I heard the awesome rumbling of great power. I saw Jesus in the clouds, and He told me He had a work for me to do.

Since this experience, I have learned from my studies about God riding on a cherub. It is their wings flapping that makes that awesome sound.

Thank You, Lord, because You heard my prayer, and I have seen You. Job 42:5-6 says:

> *I have heard of You by the hearing of the ear,*
> *But now my eye sees You.*
> *Therefore I abhor myself,*
> *And repent in dust and ashes.*

I pray that all who read this will do likewise. God chose me, His servant, to reveal some things that He is doing or will do in the future, and He gave me a scripture to confirm what He was asking me to do as a seer:

> *The word that came to Jeremiah from the LORD saying, "Thus speaks the LORD God of Israel, saying: 'Write in a book for yourself all the words that I have spoken to you.'"* Jeremiah 30:1-2

As I write these, His revelations, I pray that there be nothing of my own, only what is from Him. Help me, Lord, to do Your will, not mine.

Apostle Robert Delgado

CHAPTER 1

THE PROPHETIC DREAM OF TELEVISION FULFILLED

And from the days of John the Baptist until now the kingdom of heaven suffers violence, and the violent take it by force. Matthew 11:12

In 1984, when we started our pastorship, God gave me a dream. I saw a huge satellite dish, and God told me that I would be on television. Six years later, a prophet friend, George Rojas, was with us in our home, and he began to prophesy. He prophesied many things, but the thing I remember most about his prophecy was that I was going to be on television and would not have to pay anything for the time. He hadn't known anything about the dream the Lord gave me.

Five more years went by and in January of 1995, I was completely discouraged and spoke seriously with God. I had written down the Vision for our church, and it had seven points. I told God that I had been confessing this Vision now for eleven years to our church and others, but not one point of it had been fulfilled. He knew my heart, that I was not a person who liked to deceive others. I told Him that if He did not fulfill even one point of the vision, I would leave the ministry, and I gave Him one month to fulfill that one point.

I had never spoken to God in this way, and I felt bad about it, but I didn't know what to do. Then, God woke me up one night soon afterward with this scripture:

> *And from the days of John the Baptist until now the Kingdom of heaven suffers violence, and the violent take it by force.* Matthew 11:12

I felt relieved. Thank God!

In February of 1995, Jonas Gonzales, President of Channel 23 in Costa Rica, named me as the Coordinator for Spanish Christian Programing for Latin America at Channel 14, Trinity Broadcasting Network in Houston, Texas. This appointment was authorized by Dr. Paul F. Crouch, then President of Trinity Broadcasting. I accepted the position and worked there for the next sixteen years. During that time, I did not have to pay a single dime for air time. We were subsidized by the local TBN station and included in their budget. Glory to God! We recorded our programs there at the TBN studio and sent them to Channel 23 to be aired from San Jose, Costa Rica, all over Latin America.

Through this divine experience, I was being fine-tuned to the voice of God, to be His seer, just as Samuel when he was a boy:

Therefore Eli said to Samuel [after the third time God had called the lad], "Go, lie down; and it shall be, if He calls you, that you must say, 'Speak, LORD, for Your servant hears.'"

So, Samuel went and lay down in his place. Now the LORD came and stood and called as at other times, "Samuel! Samuel!"

And Samuel answered, "Speak, for Your servant hears."   1 Samuel 3:9-10

This is the life of the seer.

CHAPTER 2

WE WRESTLE NOT AGAINST...

For we do not wrestle against flesh and blood, but against principalities, against powers, against the rulers of the darkness of this age, against spiritual hosts of wickedness in the heavenly places.

Ephesians 6:12

This scripture formed the basis for the miraculous calling of my wife, Prophetess Linda Delgado, and myself to ministry. At that moment, we did yet understand what it all meant and what our calling would entail. Still, we were obedient to the calling, even if it seemed strange to us. We understood that it was totally God's doing, and we gave Him all the glory.

The first time we were in a situation that affected the spiritual atmosphere over a region was in April of 1999. We had been invited to Blue Springs, Missouri, by Pastor Dan Bohler, to minister in his Anglo church. He had seen me share my prophetic dream on the live "Praise the Lord" program with Dr. Paul F. Crouch in the TV station in Dallas. I was with Dr. Crouch three times on the program in Dallas, but this was the first time I had ministered in a White church. Up until then, I had always ministered to Hispanic congregations.

During those days, God gave me a word for the American Midwest. It was from the Scriptures:

> *Then the men of the city said to Elisha, "Please notice, the situation of the city is pleasant, as my lord sees; but the water is bad, and the ground barren."*
> *And he said, "Bring me a new bowl, and put salt in it." So, they brought it to him.*

Then he went out to the source of the water, and cast in the salt there, and said, "Thus says the LORD: 'I have healed this water; from it there shall be no more death or barrenness.'" So, the water remains healed to this day, according to the word which he spoke.

2 Kings 2:19-22

The Midwest is known as "the Breadbasket of the World." If it were not for politics, the entire world could be fed by the amount of grain that is grown there. The Lord said that the water represented the Word of God:

That He might sanctify and cleanse her [the Church] with the washing [you need water to wash] by the word [the Word of God]. Ephesians 5:26

But just as rivers get polluted in the natural, the Word of God, in this particular area of America, had been polluted by false doctrines, and therefore the Midwest was barren and dead spiritually. False doctrines

25

like Wicca, Free Masonry, Illuminati, Mormonism, Jehovah Witnesses, and others had polluted the Word of God. But, God said, He was bringing a cleansing of His Word through the work of the Holy Spirit.

A true move of God would sweep across Middle America like a wildfire. It had already started and would increase in size, to bring about lasting results in the spiritual life of the Midwest, the rest of America, and eventually the world.

Ministries like that of Apostle David Taylor with Joshua Media Ministries, Pastor Rod Parsley Ministries, International House of Prayer with Pastor Mike Bickle, Christian Family Church with Pastor Tim Peterson, Trinity Broadcasting Network, Daystar Television, and other Spirit-filled ministries were bringing healing to the people and to the land. Praise God!

While we were in Blue Springs, several members of the church took us to Franklin, Missouri, where there was a move of the Holy Spirit in progress. This move of God shifted to Kansas City, and is now known as

The International House of Prayer (IHOP), with Pastor Mike Bickle. God has been moving there now for several years, and this is affecting Kansas City, the state of Missouri, the Midwest, America, and the world.

At that time, I was also able to share the prophetic word that God had given me for the region on the local TBN station in Saint Joseph, Missouri.

At that same time, some friends invited us to go minister in Minnesota and Wisconsin. While we were in Eau Claire, Wisconsin, we were led by the Spirit to do a prophetic act like Elisha. Let's look at that passage again:

> *Then the men of the city said to Elisha, "Please notice, the situation of this city is pleasant, as my lord sees; but the water is bad, and the ground is barren."*
> *And he said, "Bring me a new bowl, and put salt in it." So, they brought it to him. Then he went out to the source of the water, and cast in the salt there, and said, "Thus says the LORD: 'I have healed this water; from it there shall be*

> *no more death or barrenness.'" So, the*
> *water remains healed to this day, ac-*
> *cording to the word of Elisha which he*
> *spoke.*   2 Kings 2:19-22

We bought a new bowl, put salt in it, and went to downtown Eau Claire, where two rivers meet. They are the Eau Claire River and the Chippewa River.

To God be the glory, after we did that prophetic act, that part of the downtown of Eau Claire, which was the Skid Row of the city at the time, began to prosper. It is newly developed and beautified. This is what God is going to do throughout the Midwest and the rest of America.

Our friends, like Judy and Steve Holm, Robert and Pauline Hays from Chippewa Falls, Wisconsin, Susan Campbell-Paulson from Eau Claire, and others can testify to this transformation that took place after that prophetic act.

During this time, we also ministered in Barron, Wisconsin. We stayed at the home of the president of the Women's Aglow for the state. The Sunday before we went to stay with her there had been a severe storm in the area. That Monday morning I was awakened by the Holy Spirit. We were sleeping in a bedroom in the basement, and the window of the bedroom was on ground level. I saw what I thought was a lot of lightning. I thought it was another storm, but when I opened the blinds, I saw that it was a beautiful, clear day. The Holy Spirit told me it was "War."

This was in the spring of the year 2000, before the events of 9/11. At the time of this writing, we have now in a series of wars, in Iraq, Afghanistan, and Syria for the past twenty-three years. While we were in Barren, I prophesied that Barron would not be barren anymore!

On another trip to Minnesota, we ministered at a multiracial church. At the beginning of the service God gave me a word of knowledge. The Lord said, "There is a woman here wearing a wig. Her hair is falling out because she has some kind of disease." A woman came forward from the back of the church. I asked if that was she, and she said, "Yes." I noticed that she was wearing a wig. I asked her if she was saved, and she said "No." I led her to Christ and prayed for her healing.

Later that night I asked the lady what type of disease she had suffered from. She said, "I have lupus."

I said, "No, you *had* lupus."

She said again, "I have lupus."

I said, "No, you *had* lupus."

Understanding now, she said, "O, yes, I *had* lupus." She was healed from lupus and her pastor, Joe Sutton, confirmed it.

Next, the Holy Spirit turned our focus to Latin America, to the changing of the spiritual atmosphere in certain regions of influence from the power of darkness to the Light.

CHAPTER 3

POR AMOR A TABASCO
(FOR THE LOVE OF TABASCO)

If My people who are called by My name will humble themselves, and pray and seek My face, and turn from their wicked ways, then I will hear from heaven, and will forgive their sin and heal their land.   2 Chronicles 7:14

In 2004, the Governor of the State of Tabasco in Mexico asked the evangelical churches in that area to help combat an epidemic of youth suicides. Coming from a Catholic governor, this was considered very unprofessional, but he did it anyway. His campaign was called, "POR AMOR

A TABASCO" (FOR THE LOVE OF TABASCO).

The State of Tabasco is divided into seventeen municipalities, and therefore, seventeen different international evangelical ministries were invited to hold a week-long campaign in each of the seventeen municipalities simultaneously. We were asked to hold our ministry in the municipality of Jalpa De Mendez.

Four small churches helped to back the event with Pastor Jose Trinidad Martinez of Iglesia Torre Fuerte (Strong Tower Church), Pastor Jose Jimenez of Iglesia Monte Horeb (Mount Horeb Church), Pastor Amadio Garcia of Iglesia Monte De Los Olivos (Mount of Olives Church), and Pastor Santiago Marin. All these churches are now very prominent in the municipality. To God be the glory for the transformation of the atmosphere against the spirit of suicide over Jalpa De Mendez Municipality, the State of Tabasco, and for its prosperity! The State of Tabasco is now number one in the number of evangelicals in the nation of Mexico, and that spirit of suicide was defeated.

We cannot take the credit for this transformation. It took the effort of all the ministries, churches, and us, God's servants, to be obedient to His calling to perform His work for the people of Tabasco, and especially, their governor who cried out to God for help. Praise God!

During one of our trips to Tabasco, I was ministering at one of the churches that sponsored us, Iglesia Monte Horeb (Mount Horeb Church), with Pastor Josue Jimenez. We had a glorious service.

After the service, a young mother brought me her newborn baby girl so I could pray for her. She had been born with a deformed rectum and was not able to defecate. I prayed for the baby, and we returned to the U.S. That following year we returned and learned that God had performed a creative miracle on that child. The baby girl defecated the day after I had prayed for her, and she is completely healed to this day. Hallelujah!

CHAPTER 4

MISSION NICARAGUA

And a vision appeared to Paul in the night. A man of Macedonia stood and pleaded with him, saying, "Come over to Macedonia and help us." Acts 16:9

Also in 2004 I went to Nicaragua for the second time. I had gone the previous year by land from Punta Arenas, Costa Rica (where I had attended the Summit of TBN/ENLACE) to Managua, Nicaragua, and I was impressed with the beauty of the country of Nicaragua, especially Lake Nicaragua and a volcanic island (Ometepe), which had a perfectly-coned volcano.

Now I was flying from San Jose, Costa Rica to Managua, and I purposely sat by the window because I wanted to see that beautiful lake and the island volcano. Unfortunately, I could not see anything because it was so cloudy that day.

Just then the Holy Spirit gave me a word for Nicaragua. He said there was going to be a revolution in Nicaragua, not a revolution of Socialism, not a revolution of Communism, but a revolution of a great move of God, and men of God would take this revolution to the other nations.

This move of God was brought about by the members of Full Gospel Business Men's Fellowship International, which evangelized that whole nation with signs and wonders following, through what they called, "Fire Teams." Hallelujah!

Yes, I do believe (and say it humbly) that our being called by God to these regions has affected their spiritual atmosphere, but God receives all the glory. We are just His instruments.

One testimony I heard that took place during this move of God in Nicaragua was outstanding. There had been a civil war in the country between the government and the Sandinistas in the 1980s, which ended in 1990. At one of the meetings of the FGMFI, the men from either side of the conflict were asking forgiveness of each other. One of the government soldiers had been captured and tortured by the Sandinistas. They had cut off his tongue, and when they were asking forgiveness of each other in that service, God grew out that man's tongue, and He was able to speak again. That miracle brought forgiveness and unity to those previous enemies. Praise God!

In the August 2005 edition of *Charisma* magazine, the headline was, "A New Revolution in Nicaragua." Sure enough, this revolution was not of Socialism, nor of Communism, but a true move of God! God confirms His Word. Amen!

CHAPTER 5

ONE MEXICO, ONE PRAYER
(UN MEXICO, UNA ORACIÓN)

*But where sin abounded, Grace abound-
ed much more.*   Romans 5:20

In January of 2009, I was made aware
by the Holy Spirit of a furious attack by
the forces of darkness against the nation
of Mexico through the wars perpetrated
by the drug cartels against each other,
against the government authorities, and
against innocent people. This was affecting the very fiber of decency and morality
of this beautiful nation in every segment
of their society. Unfortunately, it is still
an ongoing war. Thank God for His grace
that abounds.

We were led to call the Church in Mexico to spiritual warfare. At the time, I was working as Coordinator of Spanish Christian Programming here in Houston, Channel 14 with TBN/ENLACE, and I felt strongly led to use the network of ENLACE to form a united campaign to combat the forces of evil through unified prayer.

Jonas Gonzales, Jr., President of ENLACE, told me to contact Luis Marroquin, Director of ENLACE in Mexico City, which I did, and he ran with it to form the, "UN MEXICO, UNA ORACIÓN" (ONE MEXICO, ONE PRAYER) campaign against violence in Mexico.

The strategy was to unite the Church in Mexico and have prayer services in all the main cities of the nation and then end it with one large gathering at the main square (El Zocalo) in downtown Mexico City in front of the seat of government. During the campaign, more than a million Mexican Evangelical Christians united in prayer for Mexico and more than 70,000 gathered in Mexico City to pray for Mexico. My wife and I were privileged to be among them. Since then, the violence has diminished, but we are believing for a complete transformation of Mexico through the work of the Holy Spirit and His Church. There is a strong devil that does not want to give up, but he is defeated. You will read more about him in this book. He is called "La Santa Muerte."

CHAPTER 6

THE CAMPAIGN AGAINST VIOLENCE, EL SALVADOR
(LA CAMPAÑA CONTRA LA VIOLENCIA, EL SALVADOR)

If My people [the Church] who are called by My name will humble them- selves, and pray and seek My face, and turn from their wicked ways, then I will hear from heaven, and will forgive their sin and heal their land.

2 Chronicles 7:14

In April of 2014, my wife and I went to minister at Iglesia Del Camino (Church On the Way), Ciudad Merliot, El Salvador with Pastor Mauricio Navas. I had ministered there previously, but I was not aware that we were going to take part in the nation's, "Campaign Against Violence." The pastor had not told me till we got there, but God knew.

The same strategy was applied here that was done in Mexico. The churches were holding city-wide services and praying to combat violence that was horribly affecting the whole nation. The Church in El Salvador led by Pastor Mauricio Navas has been praying for their country for fourteen years now.

The first time I ministered at Pastor Navas' church, I gave him a word with three parts: First, that He was going to minister to a mass of people. Later, he was invited to preach at the National Stadium to more than 100,000 people.

Second, that television would open up to him. When the civil war ended, each opposing side got a TV station. The Sandinistas did not know what to do with theirs, so they gave it to Pastor Navas.

Third, that radio would open up for them, and that also happened. To God be the glory! This all happened within one year.

This was the first time the Holy Spirit had allowed me to tell any church (and, mind you, this was an Assembly of God Church) that people had seen angels when I minister. We had a glorious service, and the pastor took me out to eat.

That evening, before the service, the pastor told me that a very prominent and mature Christian member of their church had told him he saw angels all around the ceiling of the sanctuary holding golden trumpets. Hallelujah! This has since happened repeatedly in other churches.

In 2014, God gave me a word for the nation that there was going to be a move of God, that El Salvador would prosper abundantly, and that those who had left the country would return when they heard that there was bread (prosperity) in El Salvador again. This reminded me of what happened with Naomi and Ruth:

Then she arose with her daughters-in-law that she might return from the country of Moab, for she had heard in the country of Moab that the LORD had visited His people by giving them bread.   Ruth 1:6

God is still in the process of doing something great in El Salvador. He has united the churches, and as of this writing they have a new president that is willing to confront corruption and violence. I have even heard testimonies and seen videos of a move of God in the prisons among the Mara Salvatrucha gang, the 18th Street gang, and others. Hallelujah! We continue to pray for these regions, for there to be a mighty move of God that will transform the whole land and their people.

Again:

Surely the LORD God does nothing, Unless He reveals His secrets to His servants the prophets.   Amos 3:7

Next, I am going to mention specific prophetic words that were given to me by the Holy Spirit to fulfill specific purposes of God that are unique in nature and urgent. My desire is that these prophetic words from God will strengthen you and encourage you to move with zeal to be about the Father's business.

CHAPTER 7

PRELUDE TO A PROPHETIC DREAM

Then he dreamed, and a ladder was set up on the earth, and its top reached to heaven; and there the angels of God were ascending and descending on it.

Genesis 28:12

What I am about to share is not to boast in the least. As I have said previously, we are just God's humble servants, and the glory is His alone. This prophetic dream came with the manifestation of angels, just like biblical events in both the Old and New Testaments, One example would be Jacob in Genesis 28:12. Here are a few other examples:

GIDEON

And the Angel of the LORD appeared to him and said to him, "The LORD is with you, you mighty man of valor!"

Judges 6:12

DANIEL

And the prince of the kingdom of Persia withstood me twenty-one days; and behold, Michael, one of the chief princes, came to help me, for I had been left alone there with the kings of Persia.

Daniel 10:13

MARY, AT THE BIRTH OF JESUS

Now in the sixth month the angel Gabriel was sent by God to a city of Galilee named Nazareth, to a virgin betrothed to a man whose name was Joseph, of the house of David. The virgin's name was Mary. Luke 1:26-27

THE SHEPHERDS IN THE FIELD

*And suddenly there was with the angel
a multitude of the heavenly host prais-
ing God and saying…* Luke 2:13

And there were many others.

A few days before I received the prophetic dream, I had a visitation from angels. It was in the first week of September 1995, the night before we started our production week at Channel 14 TBN station, Houston.

That Sunday night, at 3 AM I was awakened from sleep by a bang on our bedroom window, accompanied by the sound of a strong wind blowing. I thought it was a storm, but the Holy Spirit told me it was angels doing spiritual warfare on my behalf. I said, "I'm tired. They can handle it. I'm going back to sleep."

That Monday afternoon at 1:30 PM, we started production. Pastor Francisco Orantes, visiting for the first time from El Salvador, was in the studio as a guest. When he saw me, he told me he had dreamed

51

about me that night. He said he saw me behind the pulpit dressed as a prince holding a sword in my right hand. Using that sword, I was dividing the clouds. He said after a while I got tired and lowered the sword, but two angels came from behind and lifted my arms.

The Holy Spirit gave him the interpretation, which had two meanings. First, he said, there was strong spiritual warfare being waged in the air against the wicked host on my behalf. Second, God was soon going to bless our ministry and many great things that had never been seen before were going to be seen.

THE PROPHETIC DREAM

One night in September of 1995, I was sleeping soundly when I had a dream from God. The dream consisted of three scenes. In the first scene, I saw a lady I had met a few years earlier in our church. Her name was Claudia Benitez, and she was a missionary from Guatemala to the Philippines. In the dream, she was using sign language and relating a miracle that was taking place at that moment. A man with a withered right arm was being miraculously healed in the name of Jesus in front of everyone. I understood that this was being televised live, and the Spirit said, "Israel."

The second scene began, and I saw a large sanctuary with its seats arranged in a fan shape. There were people standing all around, dressed in white, waving white flags. I understood, by the Spirit, that they were fasting, and their fast was that they did not speak. I also understood that they could send signals with their flags. I could hear them groaning in their spirits. The Holy Spirit said, "Killeen, Texas."

The third scene began with a small group from our church standing in a circle. To my right was a member of our church at the time named Maritza Trevino. She started to cry and said, "I have birthed Ezekiel 39." I, too, started to cry and fell to my knees with my face to the ground. Then the rest of the people did the same.

I woke up and said, "Ezekiel what?" I heard a voice say, "39." That night I read Ezekiel 38 and 39. I already knew what they were all about, but I did not get the interpretation of the dream until a few days later in my sleep.

THE INTERPRETATION

The night the Lord revealed the interpretation of this dream, I was sleeping, and in my sleep the Lord started to reveal the meaning. I started to cry and woke up crying. I looked to see if my wife had awakened, but she had not. I got up and went into the living room where the Lord continued to reveal the interpretation to me. He said, "The three scenes are three years."

In the first year, the Lord said, there would be Christian television in Israel, and the Jews would see miracles performed in the name of Jesus. The miracle of the man with the withered arm being healed and televised is what I believe to be the sign of the start of the first year.

The second year was the most terrible to bear and made me very sad. The Lord said there would be a great slaughter of American troops in the Middle East. Killeen, Texas is where Fort Hood (recently renamed Fort Cavazos) is located, and usually the soldiers sent to the Middle East are from this particular Army Base.

On August 24, 2006, I was taking my wife to dinner in nearby Sugar Land, Texas to celebrate our 30th wedding anniversary. As I was entering the ramp to get on Interstate 69, I felt an unction of the Holy Spirit and started to weep. The Spirit let me know that the slaughter of American troops would be the sinking of an American aircraft carrier, which houses more than six thousand personnel.

The Holy Spirit said, "This great slaughter of American troops will cause public opinion to turn against us having our military in the Middle East. So, the president will be forced to pull our military out from that part of the world."

In the third year, Russia and its radical Islamic alliance will invade Israel, but God is going to destroy Russia and her radical Islamic allies on the mountains of Israel, just as is written in Ezekiel 39. In that moment, the whole world will know the God of Israel.

The Holy Spirit said, "This great victory for Israel will usher in the greatest move of the Holy Spirit on the face of the Earth. God is going to dress His Church with His glory, and the Church is going to do great signs and wonders in the name of Jesus. Every Christian is going to be instantly healed, and the elderly Christians will be rejuvenated. In this way, God is going to make a distinction between the Church and the world."

The Spirit said, "Islam is going to fall." Then I saw millions upon millions of Muslims being saved and coming to the full knowledge of our Lord Jesus Christ.

The Lord said, "Whole nations are going to be saved."

I thought in the flesh and said, "Oh yeah, like El Salvador, the smallest nation in Central America."

God rebuked me and said, "You don't think I can save America?"

I said, "I know You can save America. Save America. I love my country."

He continued, "The Mormons and the Jehovah Witnesses are going to lose so many members that their organizations will go bankrupt and collapse. Christian organizations with error in their doctrine will see their error and repent."

For the earth will be filled
With the knowledge of the glory of the
LORD,
As the waters cover the sea.
Habakkuk 2:14

The Spirit said, "The World harvest will last seven years."

The enemy who sowed them is the devil,
the harvest is the end of the age, and the
reapers are the angels. Matthew 13:39

57

Then He said, "You know what is next." All I know that is next is the Rapture of the Church of our Lord Jesus Christ.

God let me understand that during this time is when He will bring about the transfer of wealth from the sinners to the just. The Lord said He is not finished with America. Companies on Wall Street and Fortune 500 companies will give their wealth to ministries, and He said He is going to use angels to bring it about.

CHAPTER 8

GOD GAVE ME A WARNING

And He said to me, "Do not seal the words of the prophecy of this book, for the time is at hand. He who is unjust, let him be unjust still; he who is filthy, let him be filthy still; he who is righteous, let him be righteous still; he who is holy, let him be holy still.

"And behold, I am coming quickly, and My reward is with Me, to give to every one according to his work."

Revelation 22:10-12

Was this dream biblical? Yes, Ezekiel 38 and 39 speak about a future invasion of Israel by Russia (using its ancient name of Magog) and her radical Islamic allies. We thought this might have occurred during either one of the Gulf wars, but I now realize that all the players mentioned in Ezekiel were not there. Unfortunately, they are now. They are Russia (Rosh), Turkey (Meshech), Iran (Persia), Sudan/Ethiopia (Cush), and Libya (Put).

Joel 2 gives us the sequence of events. It speaks of a worldwide harvest and a worldwide move of God and of God destroying Russia and her allies:

> *"But I will remove far from you the northern army [Russia],*
> *And will drive him away into a barren and desolate land,*
> *With his face toward the eastern [Dead] sea*
> *And his back toward the western [Mediterranean] sea;*
> *His stench will come up,*
> *And his foul odor will rise,*
> *Because he has done monstrous things."*   Joel 2:20

This great victory for Israel will usher in the greatest harvest–physical (natural) and spiritual simultaneously—upon the face of the Earth. First, will come the physical harvest (prosperity):

"Fear not, O land;
Be glad and rejoice,
For the LORD *HAS done marvelous things [the destruction of Russia and its radical Islamic allies]!*
Do not be afraid, you beasts of the field.
For the open pastures are springing up,
And the tree bears its fruit;
The fig tree and the vine yield their strength.
Be glad then, you children of Zion,
And rejoice in the LORD *your God;*
For He has given you the former rain faithfully,
And He will cause the rain to come down for you —
The former rain,
And the latter rain in the first month.
The threshing floors shall be full of wheat,

And the vats shall overflow with new wine and oil.

So, I will restore to you the years that the swarming locust has eaten,

The crawly locust,

The consuming locust,

And the chewing locust,

My great army which I sent among you.

You shall eat in plenty and be satisfied,

And praise the name of the LORD your God,

Who has dealt wondrously with you;

And My people shall never be put to shame.

Then you shall know that I am in the midst of Israel:

I am the LORD your God

And there is no other.

My people shall never be put to shame.

Joel 2:21-27

Second, the spiritual harvest will come simultaneously and worldwide:

And it shall come to pass afterward [after Russia and its radical Islamic allies are destroyed]
That I will pour out My Spirit on all flesh.   Joel 2:28

In the New Testament, it says:

"And it shall come to pass in the last days [a future event]," says God,
"That I will pour out of My Spirit on all flesh;
Your sons and your daughters shall prophesy,
Your young men shall see visions,
Your old men shall dream dreams."
                                       Acts 2:17

The prophetic dream mentioned seven years of harvest and I understood seven years of famine, in accordance with Joseph's interpretation of Pharaoh's dreams:

Then Joseph said to Pharaoh, "The dreams of Pharaoh are one; God has

63

shown Pharaoh what He is about to do: The seven good cows are seven years, and the seven good heads are seven years; the dreams are one. And the seven thin and ugly cows which came up after them are seven years, and the seven empty heads blighted by the east wind are seven years of famine [the future seven years of the Tribulation after the harvest]. This is the thing which I have spoken to Pharaoh. God has shown Pharaoh what He is about to do.

Genesis 41:25-28

God had spoken to His seer of what He was about to do.

Amazingly, something glorious happens between the great harvest and the Tribulation—the Rapture of the Universal Church of Jesus Christ! Just as Joseph brought his family [Israel] to Egypt to escape death from famine and Pharaoh ordered Joseph to put Jacob and his family in the best location in Egypt–the land of Goshen (a land of plenty and comfort)—God has a safe place for the Church during the seven years of Tribulation, and that is in Heaven with Jesus. Let's look again at Matthew 13:39:

The enemy who sowed them is the devil, the harvest is the end of the age, and the reapers are the angels [messengers].

This scripture is specific that the end-time harvest indicates the end of the age. This most likely refers to the end of the Church age or the end of the age of grace, which are the same, but with different names.

Another scripture that references the end-time move of God is Acts 3:19-21:

Repent therefore and be converted, that your sins may be blotted out, so that times of refreshing [Joel 2:28-29 fulfilled in Acts 2:1-4] may come from the presence of the Lord, and that He may send Jesus Christ, who was preached to you before, whom heaven must receive until the times of restoration of all things [the seven-year world harvest and the greatest move of the Holy Spirit on the face of the Earth], which God has spoken by the mouth of all His holy prophets since the world began.

This is confirmation of the final move of God upon the Church of Jesus Christ to bring about the renewal of the Church, the preparation of Christ's Bride [the Church], and the great end-time harvest. Even so, come, Lord Jesus!

IN CONCLUSION

That He might present her to Himself
a glorious church, not having, spot or
wrinkle or any such thing, but that she
should be holy and without blemish.
                                    Ephesians 5:27

We are at the threshold of the greatest move of God the Earth has ever seen. There will be astronomical changes occurring in the Church. Compared to the Church that we see today, the revived Church will be unrecognizable.

The Holy Spirit will do a quick work to prepare the Church for her Groom—Jesus Christ. This latter move of God will be greater than the book of Acts and the Azusa

Street Revival. The fivefold ministry, as recorded in Ephesians 4:11-13, is God's divine order of things:

And He Himself gave some to be apostles, some prophets, some evangelists, and some pastors and teachers, for the equipping of the saints for the work of ministry, for the edifying of the body of Christ, till we all come to the unity of the faith and of the knowledge of the of the Son of God, to the measure of the stature of the fullness of Christ.

This divine order will be in full force, but signs, wonders, and miracles will not be limited to ministers only. They will be experienced by the whole Body of Christ, the Church Universal, to bring in the world harvest. The apostles, prophets, evangelist, pastors, and teachers are the government, or authority, of the Church, and they will train the saints for the work of the ministry:

For the perfecting of the saints, for the work of the ministry, for the edifying of the body of Christ.

There will be much more order and re-spect for authority than there currently is today. The purpose of this divine order of ministry is clear:

For the edifying of the body of Christ, till we all come to the unity of the faith and of the knowledge of the Son of God, to a perfect man, to the measure of the stature of the fullness of Christ.

The whole Church will recognize God's divine order and will flow together in unity to accomplish His purposes.

All the miracles that you read about in the Old Testament and the New Testament will be now mega in size and magnitude during this seven-year period of harvest. We have never been this way before, but it will be glorious!

THE LAST TEN YEARS OF CHURCH HISTORY BEFORE THE RAPTURE

The first year: Christian television in Israel and the miracle of the man with the withered right arm healed in the sight of everyone in the name of Jesus will be the start of the ten-year period of events leading up to the Rapture of the Church of Jesus Christ.

The second year will see the slaughter of American troops in the Middle East mentioned on page 51.

During the third year, the destruction by God of Russia and her radical Islamic allies on the mountains of Israel will take place, just as is described in Ezekiel 39.

The last seven years will be years of world harvest and the greatest move of the Holy Spirit on the face of the Earth ever. At the end of the ten years, the Rapture of the glorious Church of Jesus Christ will take place!

Get Ready!
Get Ready!
Get Ready!

For yet a little while,
And He [Jesus Christ] who is coming will
come and will not tarry! **Hebrews** 10:37

CHAPTER 10

TWO MORE REVELATIONS, THESE FOR THE UNBELIEVER

For God has not given us a spirit of fear, but of power and of love and of a sound mind. 2 Timothy 1:7

I have two more revelations God has given me with profound consequences for the unbeliever. Read them and meditate on them, for God does not want His Church to be ignorant of these things.

THE DIVINE MANIFESTATION

In the spring of 2004, my wife and I went to California. I was going to minister at my brother-in law's Spanish Assembly of God church in the lovely town of Ontario.

That Sunday morning, during the praise and worship service, I was standing and singing with the congregation when the floor underneath my feet started to roll like waves. I didn't say anything, but the rolling continued. Furthermore, it made me dizzy.

My brother-in-law, Pastor Robert Almendariz, asked me to greet the church from the pulpit, so I walked up to the front of the church to the podium, and I continued to feel the rolling of the floor.

After church, I asked my wife and her sister, Ruth Almendariz, the pastor's wife, if they had felt the floor moving. My wife said she had, but my sister-in-law said she hadn't felt anything. The manifestation lasted for thirty to forty-five minutes.

I didn't think at the time that this was a divine manifestation until God gave me the interpretation a few days later. God said the floor rolling underneath my feet spoke of a devastating earthquake that would hit California. It would be the worst earthquake in modern history. It would last thirty to forty-five minutes and cause great devastation. This event would be in the news for weeks and even months worldwide.

God told me the earthquake would occur on a Sunday the 29th, but He didn't give me the month or the year. This might come in a future revelation. It's all up to God.

God said this is when He will make a distinction between His children and the world. The Church does not have to fear the quake, because it will not affect them. To God be the glory! O, mighty God, Your judgments are just and righteous altogether. Amen!

A similar deliverance happened to the children of Israel while they were in Egypt and is recorded in the book of Exodus:

> *But against none of the children of Israel shall a dog move its tongue, against man or beast, that you may know that the LORD does make a difference between the Egyptians and Israel.* Exodus 11:7

God destroyed Egypt with the plagues that occurred over their land. However, the plagues did not touch the Israelites, and they were able to plunder Egypt. In this way, God gave His people a great deliverance.

The Word of God says that every matter is confirmed by two or three witnesses:

> *This will be the third time I am coming to you. "By the mouth of two or three witnesses every word shall be established."* 2 Corinthians 13:1

God confirmed this revelation by three witnesses:

THE FIRST WITNESS

I had sent out copies of this divine manifestation to different ministries. A few days later, a pastor, Juan Ruiz Jr., from Delaney, California, wrote to me and told me they had received the letter I sent them on Thursday. He and his wife read it but did not mention it to anybody else. Then, on

Friday, when he got home from his office, his wife was on the phone with a lady from their church, and she was very emotional. His wife handed him the phone so that he could hear what the lady was saying.

The lady was sharing a dream she'd had. In the dream, she was at the church on the second floor with her two daughters when the building started shaking and the floors rolling. Then the building started to fall apart. She helped her daughters down, but she herself remained hanging from a staircase. Her husband helped her down.

She said the earthquake lasted thirty to forty-five minutes. They were outside when a family member drove up, and they left in his car. Then she woke up.

THE SECOND WITNESS

During the production of our Spanish TV programs, one of our guests was from Los Angeles. He had been a well-known child evangelist, but now he was a teenager. I shared with him this divine manifestation. He said his mother had had a dream of a terrible earthquake that hit California. It lasted thirty to forty-five minutes, and California became islands, and those islands were churches!

Pray for California. She has sown the wind and must reap the whirlwind of destruction. She has mocked God, and God cannot be mocked.

THE UNGODLY GLORIFICATION OF DEATH

The ungodly glorification of death is called, "LA SANTA MUERTE" (HOLY DEATH), in Mexico. There is absolutely nothing "HOLY" about death. In fact, death is the second enemy of humanity mentioned in the Bible after Satan:

> *But of the tree of the knowledge of good and evil you shall not eat, for the day that you eat of it you shall surely die [death entered the picture].*
>
> Genesis 2:17

The angel of death is so powerful that it will be the last enemy of humanity that will be destroyed by God:

Then Death and Hades were cast into the lake of fire. This is the second death.
Revelation 20:14

The glorification of this fallen angel has now come to the United States of America from Mexico, and because of America's greed for the mighty dollar, it is now being hailed and promulgated through the fashion industry, marketing, and the media. Tragically, people don't seem to understand that this has brought a curse to our land. The occult is behind this onslaught.

We have great and clear examples in history where this devil has been glorified and the consequences have been disastrous. We have the example of the pirates and their emblem of the skull and cross bones. Where are they now?

The greatest example is Nazi Germany, and Hitler's involvement in the occult, with its storm troopers and the skulls on their uniforms and the dreaded SS Troopers with their skull tattoos and hats. Just look at the damning results to the whole country of Germany and the world through World War II!

And yet, today we can look at our neighbor to our south and see what is happening to beautiful Mexico. From the highest level of the government to the least peasant, we see a foolish glorification of "LA SANTA MUERTE" and can also see what diabolical havoc this demon is causing in that country. There are altars, covenants, and worship of this entity, and we can see the results: corruption in every area of society, a pandemic of crime, murders, shedding of innocent blood, and social unrest in every segment of society.

In many areas, La Santa Muerte is now more venerated than the Virgin Mary. If this extreme comes to America, this devil will take complete control. We must recognize this danger and act now before it's too late.

The Holy Spirit gave me an analogy of this diabolical seduction. It is like the black widow spider. She seduces her victims with riches, fame, sex, and power for a season, but in her underbelly she has the design of an hour glass, and this is symbolic of her deception. When she is finished with her victims, she drives her poison fangs into them and destroys them and their surroundings. Their time is up, and a victim never knows how much time she will permit them. They are left fools.

Fellow Americans, we can turn things around. Our country is in danger of destruction. Why? Because we have allowed the glorification of this demon in our country. What can we do? Church, you have the authority and we know the Answer.

Again, God said:

If my people who are called by My name will humble themselves, and pray and seek My face, and turn from their wicked ways, then I will hear

> *from heaven, and will forgive their sin*
> *and heal their land.*2 Chronicles 7:14

We can start by boycotting all products, businesses, and merchandise that bear a skull and glorify death.

You might think this is too simplistic, but God never asks us to do anything that is too hard for us to do. For example, He had the people of Israel march around Jericho, and the walls came falling down. He ordered King Jehoshaphat to place the choir in front of the army of Israel, and God gave them a great victory over insurmountable the numbers coming against them. In both situations, all it took was obedience. The Church united can accomplish this and much more.

Again, the Word of God says that every matter is confirmed by two or three witnesses. God again confirmed this revelation by three witnesses:

THE FIRST WITNESS: I shared with a group of pastors who are my partners in prayer weekly on Mondays here in

Rosenberg, Texas. Pastor Claude Villemaire was pastor of a local Lutheran Church at the time. He shared that a Hispanic woman had visited their church one Sunday morning. She said there were weird things happening in her house and she wanted them to go there and pray. The pastor went with several of his members to pray for her house.

They looked to see if there was anything in the house that might open the door to the occult. At first, they didn't find anything, but the pastor felt to look further. He looked inside a closet, and when he did, he found an altar to La Santa Muerte hidden in the interior of the closet.

THE SECOND WITNESS: My son, Pastor Robert Phillip Delgado, was, for a time, a paramedic for the Houston Fire Department. He told me they were called to a murder scene at some apartments. A man had been viciously murdered in a drug-related incident. It was a horrible murder. When they went into the murdered man's bedroom they saw all kinds of paraphernalia of the occult and an altar to La Santa Muerte.

THE THIRD WITNESS: I called Cesar Español of TBN/ENLACE to let him know what the Holy Spirit had revealed to me about La Santa Muerte and its affect in Mexico. When I heard from him again, he told me that a very prominent pastor from Brazil had called him right after I hung up with him and wanted to know why Mexico was so bewitched by this devil of La Santa Muerte.

Remember Paul's words to Timothy:

> *For God has not given us a spirit of fear, but of power and of love and of a sound mind.* 2 Timothy 1:7

The devil is a defeated foe, for it is written:

> *I will build My church, and the gates of Hades shall not prevail against it.* Matthew 16:18

Yes, we have the victory through our Lord Jesus Christ! Amen!

Author Contact

You may contact Apostle Robert Delgado in the following ways:

Email: delgarob@aol.com

Cellphone: 832-788-4196

www.ingramcontent.com/pod-product-compliance
Lightning Source LLC
LaVergne TN
LVHW011215080426
835508LV00007B/810